*The much-loved landmark of Bidston windmill.*

# WIRRA
## AN I

The Wirral Peninsula – better known to many as 'Wirral' or 'The Wirral' – is that tongue of land bounded by the Rivers Mersey and Dee and the Irish Sea. It's a region that has managed to retain its identity as 'a place apart', a unique part of England at the hub of the British Isles, with wonderful western vistas of Welsh wildernesses, fabulous sunsets over Irish Sea horizons, and at its doorstep two of Britain's best cities – Chester and Liverpool.

Within its small area of about eighteen miles by eight is a community of people who live in pleasant and varied towns and suburbs, villages and hamlets set in a rich and varied landscape of well-tended countryside and with a forty-mile coastline unsurpassed in its variety – in fact it's an England in miniature!

Add to that a people who are proud of their identity as Wirralians and who are friendly and yet jealously guard their beloved peninsula from undesirable change – and you have a place that few folk willingly leave and always return to with a feeling of 'coming home' to somewhere very special indeed.

This book encapsulates, in photographs and text, some of the places that make the Wirral Peninsula such a fascinating place.

Concept and project management by Iain Corlett.
Photographs by Guy Huntington.
Text, layout, typesetting and proofreading by Kenneth Burnley.
All material in this publication is copyright © Kenneth Burnley and Guy Huntington.
First published November 2007 by Mill Hill Publishing Ltd.
Email: enquiries@millhillpublishing.co.uk
ISBN: **978-0-9557724-0-5**
Printed by Printfine, Liverpool.

*A Mersey ferryboat berths at Woodside Ferry, the world-famous Liverpool skyline a fitting backdrop to this well-loved Wirral scene. There has been a ferry service between the Cheshire and Lancashire shores of the Mersey since the time of King John.*

The Wirral Peninsula is a place apart, somewhere regarded by its residents as 'somewhere special'. Why? Probably because it is a peninsula – indeed, almost an island. It's a west-coast place, a finger of land oriented north-west, its past influenced hugely by its setting – sandwiched not only between England and Wales, with Ireland and the Isle of Man on the distant sea horizons, but also between the world-class cities of Chester and Liverpool.

Almost surrounded by water, Wirral is a maritime place. Many residents live near the coast, or make their living from maritime occupations, or spend their recreation time by the sea. The peninsula's past has been shaped by the sea, with early settlers landing on its shores from lands far away and imprinting their ways of life onto the landscape. Through the ages the men and women of Wirral

*The River Dee and the weir at Chester. The peninsula's history and development owe much to this ancient city on Wirral's doorstep.*

have shaped their lives around the sea that laps its shores, lives that have been often enriched by its bounty, and lives that have sometimes been saddened by its violence.

Today, the influence of the sea upon the peninsula and its people is less than in former times; but its beauty, its sunsets, its continual presence on three sides of this place that so many call home, are among many reasons why Wirral folk believe that this is a 'special place'; and it's also the reason why so many come here to live and work, and why so many come here as visitors to enjoy the unique experience of peninsular life.

*Hoylake seen from the air. An ebbing tide leaves the vast expanses of sand glistening in the morning sunlight. At this northwestern tip of Wirral is Red Rocks, and a mile offshore is Hilbre Island. The Royal Liverpool Golf Course was hosting the Open Golf Championship at the time of this photo.*

Nowhere in Wirral are you more than about three or four miles from the coast. The peninsula has some forty miles of coastline – with something of interest every step of the way: a wonderful mixture of natural clay-cliffs, dunes and sandstone bluffs, sandy beaches, promenades, embankments and artificial sea defences, commerce, resorts, towns, villages and ancient ports. And always, the sight, sound and smells of the sea and its associated wildlife.

The peninsula's eastern coastline follows the bank of the Mersey for eighteen miles or so – from the petrochemical works of Stanlow to its estuarine tip at New Brighton. This is very much a man-made coast with commerce and suburbia never far away, but with here and there, at places like Eastham,

*Liverpool is prominent from most parts of Wirral's eastern coastline, but especially from Wallasey and Birkenhead.*

a glimpse of rocky sandstone cliffs and trees dipping branches into the water. All along the way are tangible reminders of Wirral's development over the centuries, from the ancient stones of Birkenhead Priory to the faded Victorian elegance of Rock Park, the remarkable garden village of Port Sunlight and Wallasey's dormitory architecture.

The city of Liverpool, with its recognisable seafront buildings, ridge-top cathedrals and crane-silhouettes of new building is a prominent

accompaniment right up to New Brighton – with occasional glimpses of the famous Mersey ferryboats plying their way across and along the river.

At New Brighton the coastline does a sharp left-turn at the entrance to the Mersey, and just as suddenly the far vista changes from river-views to sea-views. This popular resort, whose fame and fortunes have been well recounted over the years, was founded by James Atherton,

The lighthouse and Fort Perch Rock Battery at New Brighton. Sentinels of the Mersey for almost 200 years, the pair announce Wirral to vessels entering the river.

The lighthouse stands on the hazardous Black Rock, on which many ships foundered before a permanent light was erected here in 1827.

The fort – nicknamed 'the Gibraltar of the Mersey' – was conceived when the threat of invasion by Napoleon was real, to protect the Port of Liverpool and the river's shipping. By the time it was built, the threat had passed, and since then the fort has stood as something of a folly. It is now a military museum.

'New Brighton, Wallasey! What happy memories the name brings back to hundreds of thousands of holidaymakers in all parts of the world who, at some period or another, have visited the resort, returning home better in health and possessing pleasant recollections of the time spent here.'
*New Brighton Official Guide, 1949*

who said in the 1830s: 'Among its other advantages may be enumerated the salubrity of the Air, the certain supply of purest Spring Water, the aspect fronting the sea, enjoying the refreshing breeze, must tend to render New Brighton a most agreeable and desirable place of resort to the Nobility and Gentry of all the neighbouring Counties'. And so it was: for a while. The Nobility and Gentry are long gone, as have the pier, the pool, and almost everything else. But thankfully the air is still salubrious, the breeze is still refreshing, and the aspect fronting the sea is still wonderful, though less so since the construction of offshore wind turbines.

The coastline is truly artificial from here for the next six or seven miles westwards towards the north-west tip of the peninsula. Much of it is wide, open promenade backed by remnants of the old grass-covered cliffline and sand dunes that in summer are bedecked with wild flowers and butterflies. Here, skylarks fill the air with their joyful and exuberant song from early in the new year right through to late summer, and hares

*The bandstand, Vale Park, New Brighton.*

scamper among the long grasses and myriad of wild flowers. Landmarks here are centuries-old Leasowe Castle and the disused lighthouse.

At Meols, where boats are usually bobbing at anchor on the high tides, the promenade continues to King's Gap at Hoylake, where the sandy beach stretches to the estuary of the River Dee, with the Hilbre Islands prominent in the near distance out on the estuary. See notice boards at West Kirby for details of how to get to these beautiful islands out in the estuary.

From the southern end of the marine lake, cliffs of boulder-clay form the coastline right down to Heswall, several miles up-river. The beaches here, for example at Caldy and Thurstaston, are generally sandy, and most have cliff-top walks. Running parallel to the coast

*Leasowe Lighthouse, one of the oldest lighthouse sites in the country. Neglected for many years, the lighthouse is now lovingly cared for by a group of Friends and is regularly opened to the public.*

*Sailing boats ready for an event on the Marine Lake, West Kirby.*

*The Dee marshes at Lower Heswall.*

here, right down to Neston where it turns inland, is the Wirral Way, a popular linear country park. Atop the cliffs at Thurstaston is the Wirral Country Park Centre, with good parking and information services and refreshments.

The cliffs and beaches peter out as Heswall is approached, and the coastline becomes distinctly marshy from here right down to Blacon Point. Along here in a few miles is Parkgate, former port for Dublin, with its buildings 'all along one side' looking out across the green marshes towards Wales.

After Parkgate, the coastline is a mixture of marsh and pastureland, often feeling remote and lonely, with a few 'civilised' interludes, such as at Ness, with its scatter of houses and popular Harp Inn. There is little sense along here of this being a coastline at all, for the sea rarely, if ever, comes up to the land: only, at very high tides, the distant sparkle of tidal water across the marshes.

Along the few miles from Burton to Blacon Point, the coastline is a 'ghost' feature: the former cliffs can be traced in places, for example at Shotwick and further on beyond Saughall towards Blacon, where few wander and only the call of the curlew breaks the silence of the vast acres of saltmarsh and reclaimed pastures – a birdwatcher's paradise.

'The inhabitants of Neston derive considerable advantage from the contiguity of Parkgate, which has of late years become a convenient and fashionable bathing place. It is also celebrated as the port for the packets for Ireland, which generally sail to that country four times a week. The houses are chiefly disposed in one long range along the Dee banks. The inhabitants derive their principal support from the expenditure of the visitants who reside here in the bathing season.'
*A description of Parkgate in 1819*

*'All on one side like Parkgate': the main street of the village. Houses, inns and shops look across thousands of acres of saltmarsh, tidal gutters and pools towards Wales. The ferry service to Dublin is long gone, as is the seashore, but Parkgate is still a favourite place for trippers to sample its famous ice-cream and shrimps.*

*Kitty's Flash, Thurstaston Hill. A wet hollow bedecked with cotton-grass and backed by gorse- and heather-clad heathland, in an amphitheatre encircled by silver birch trees. A magical place only minutes from the busy Chester highway.*

# — COUNTRYSIDE —

A casual glance at most maps of the peninsula might give a false impression of Wirral's landscape, for the shaded 'built-up' areas radiating out from Birkenhead, Wallasey and Ellesmere Port, together with smaller patches around north and west Wirral, dominate, conveying the idea that the area is almost totally built over. In fact, a large proportion of the peninsula is agricultural countryside, but there seems to be much more because many of the built-up areas have managed to retain a very rural feeling.

The best way to get a feel for Wirral's countryside is to travel north up the A540 from Chester. Within a mile or so of Chester Cross, the countryside begins, and this is the start of Wirral proper, at Mollington. Only ten miles on, at Heswall, is the rural feeling temporarily lost – and then only for a couple of miles, for the fields and hedgerows are soon regained, and the feel of the countryside continues almost to West Kirby.

The rural heart of Wirral is a typically English blend of fields, hedgerows, trees and copses set in a gently undulating land; of twisting lanes that connect small villages and farmsteads; and of a network of bridleways and field-paths that are a rambler's delight – especially those that offer glimpses of the Welsh hills away to the west.

> 'From here a final view of Eastham village crowned by the spire sets a beautiful picture in the memory. Ambling on by fragrant hedges from stile to stile over the level fields, and far removed from the dust and the taint of petrol, you pleasantly realise the attraction of Wirral pathways. In few corners of the kingdom are there busier or wider highways than those intersecting the peninsula, and in few can there be found more quiet ways and unspoiled countryside.'
>
> **M. O'Mahony, 1924**

*Bluebells at Eastham Woods.*

# — VILLAGES —

*The Dell, Port Sunlight.*

The isolated settlements of long ago are barely recognisable today, such has been the growth and expansion of the small, rural villages that once bespeckled the peninsula, kept apart and distinct by fields, pastures and heath. Drive, though, through the network of narrow, twisting lanes in central Wirral – from Willaston, through Raby, Thornton Hough, Brimstage and Storeton – and you will get a glimpse of how the area once looked.

Or take the 'old route by the Dee' – the byway west of the A540 Chester High Road – and admire the red-stone villages of Puddington, Burton, Ness, Parkgate, Gayton, Lower Heswall, Thurstaston, Caldy and old West Kirby. Here are some favourites, and some of the reasons why.

Set amidst lush pastures in the rural heart of Wirral, Thornton Hough is regarded by many as the gem of Wirral villages. On a summer's evening the village, with its parish church, blacksmith's forge and half-timbered cottages dotted picturesquely around the village green, wears an air of pastoral peace and tranquility. Yet what we see today is not ancient by any means, for most of the village was rebuilt just over 100 years ago by two men: Joseph Hirst, a retired Yorkshire woollen merchant who built the parish church, the vicarage, church school, and the group of cottages and shops behind the church.

Then in 1889 the first Viscount Leverhulme bought Thornton Manor, a large mansion on the outskirts of Thornton Hough. Within a few years of moving into the Manor he had knocked down the old village buildings and in their places he built houses like those at Port Sunlight. He also built a school, shops, a club, and a village smithy, complete with spreading chestnut tree (recently severely lopped!). The Congregational church, in imitation Norman style, was commissioned by Lever, who insisted that no expense be spared in its design.

*The Congregational Church, Thornton Hough: a 'neo-Norman' church built by the first Viscount Leverhulme to reflect the style of architecture of the Norman period.*

*Caldy Village.*

Over on the western side of Wirral is Caldy, surrounded by natural beauty: the beach and cliffs bordering the estuary are but a stone's throw away; the heathland and birch woods of Caldy Hill rise above the village; and the quiet gothic quality of Stapledon Wood (named after the writer and philosopher Olaf Stapledon) lies at the edge of the village. Edward Hubbard, the architect, summed it up in this fine description: 'By reason of its prosperous commuter country Cheshire is something of a Surrey of the north; but Surrey has nothing to compare with this.' Another local man, Norman Ellison (Nomad) summed the place up in a rather different manner: 'I ask for nothing more satisfying than a stroll before breakfast on a sunny spring morning, beneath silver birches wearing their delicate new greenery; or a brisker walk when a harvest moon is flooding the channels of the Dee with light, and borne on the still air there comes the murmur of countless seabirds seeking their supper at the edge of the ebbing tide.'

Still on the western side of Wirral, but ten miles south of Caldy, Burton is another red-sandstone village rich in history. But it was not always so. Four hundred years ago the village boasted five licensed alehouses (there are none now!) scattered along the main street. These were busy days for Burton, with trading vessels anchoring in the shelter of the rocky headland down by the Dee, and goods of every description being brought ashore for conveyance to Chester. Small wonder then that the parish church is dedicated to St Nicholas, patron saint of both mariners and moneylenders! There were probably plenty of both in medieval Burton.

There are reminders of Burton's past in every nook and cranny of the village. The cottages perched high on the outcropping sandstone along the main street testify to antiquity; search out the birthplace and home of Bishop Wilson, one-time Bishop of the Isle of Man and benefactor to Burton; consider the many building styles and materials used in the cottages; and admire the quiet beauty of the old-fashioned flower gardens.

*Top: A quiet corner of Burton village – Bishop Wilson's Cottage.*
*Below: Thornton Hall Hotel and Leisure Centre.*

Is Port Sunlight really a village? Not in the popular imagery of an English village. Yet parts of it are certainly village-like. A century ago a visitor described the place: 'How often we who love the country find rural beauty destroyed by manufactures, land bare and barren, sky dulled by smoke; look at yonder village, clean and neat; look at those roads lined with young elms and chestnuts, at the half-timbered Cheshire cottages each with its garden plot, at the stone bridge, the little church, the fine halls and the immense works. Port Sunlight is a lasting honour to the men who own it and built it.'

I go to Port Sunlight on those days in May when the blossom-trees are in full flower and the gardens are ablaze with wallflowers and tulips. It's too early in the year for the roses – that is a mid-summer treat to look forward to with anticipation. But the village on such days looks new, fresh and clean. Sunshine and shadow highlight the ornate detail of the houses, throwing the fine plasterwork into sharp relief. W. H. Lever's dream of building houses in which his work-people could 'live and be comfortable – with gardens back and front' – in which they would be able to 'know more about the science of life than they can in a back slum, and in which they will learn that there is more in life than the mere going to and returning from work' – has been fulfilled here at Port Sunlight.

> 'It is a pleasant passage over the fields to Irby. A very pretty village, in which are several picturesque old farmhouses, with many good and well-farmed acres attaching to them, where is also the Anchor Inn, with its picturesque sign of a great golden anchor swinging above the entrance.'
>
> **H. E. Young, 1909**

*Top: Christ Church, Barnston.*
*Below: Unilever works, Port Sunlight.*

*Thornton Manor, formerly the home of the Leverhulme family, now a venue for weddings and corporate functions.*

*The half-timbered beauty of the Devon Doorway at Gayton.*

What is a town? I expect there is a dictionary definition that lays down an optimum population. But to me and to many others, a town is a town by its atmosphere, its 'feel'. And so Birkenhead, Wallasey and Ellesmere Port – obviously. The modern part of Heswall feels 'towny', as do Hoylake and West Kirby, Bebington, Bromborough and Neston.

I start with the town where I was born – Wallasey. 'The Welshmen's Island' is the meaning of the name, and though it's difficult to see its island-like shape today, long ago this high mass of sandstone was indeed cut off from the rest of the peninsula. Once remote and hard to get to, the coming of the ferries and the railways brought residential development that changed the face of the place, transforming villages into the suburbia that is Wallasey today.

Separated from Wallasey by the long arm of Wallasey Pool, an inlet of the Mersey, Birkenhead is Wirral's most populous town.

*The buildings of New Brighton, dominated by the spire of St James and the dome of SS Peter and Paul, rise up from the promenade.*

*Wirral Museum (formerly Birkenhead Town Hall) and Hamilton Square.*

They used to bathe, ride donkeys, and gather periwinkles on Birkenhead beach in the olden days. That was a long time ago, of course – when meadow-lands swept down from the heights of Claughton Common, Oxton and Tranmere to the banks of the Mersey, with a tumble of rocky headlands clothed in greenery: high tides lapped against ferns and wild-flowers, and birch-branches dipped leaves and twigs into briny waters. Hard to picture it today, though. The hotels, the beaches, the greenery – it's all gone. Swept away when Laird built his shipbuilding yards here 150 years ago. That, really, was the end of the birchen heads, and the beginning of Birkenhead.

The town boasts some good buildings, the best being the former Town Hall (the Wirral Museum) in its fine setting of Hamilton Square, and the Williamson Art Gallery and Museum.

*The Williamson Art Gallery and Museum, Birkenhead.*

In the south of the peninsula, Ellesmere Port embraces lots of smaller places which have grown to become one larger entity. Village names still remind us of the scattered, agricultural and riverside communities which have been lost in recent times: Whitby, Netherpool, Overpool, Little and Great Sutton. Old guidebooks offer nostalgic glimpses of a way of life gone for ever: 'The village of Overpool, embosomed in hayricks and branches, heavy with ripening fruit'; 'Little disturbs the peace of Little Sutton except the clank of milk-cans in some paved dairy-yard, the querulous murmur of drowsy poultry, or the snip of the shears in some cottage hedgerow'. Change had to come, of course, once the canal was built. A port is a port – a place of business, activity and growth. But not just one canal came: this place boasts two canals, both designed for different purposes, but both having a dramatic effect on the growth of Ellesmere Port. All this is vividly portrayed in the Boat Museum – that tremendous achievement which has turned a run-down industrial eyesore into one of the foremost waterway experiences in the land.

*A corner of Ness Gardens.*

The first-time visitor to Wirral is usually surprised – especially if entering from the south by way of the A540 or the M53 – at the amount of open landscape. Much of this is farmed countryside, with access only by the generous range of public footpaths and bridleways. But our forebears – at least those who cared about such things, such as the pioneers of the Wirral Footpaths & Open Spaces Preservation Society, and Wirral Green Belt Council – envisioned the gradual spread of development across the peninsula and tried hard to protect the more precious bits from the hand of the builder. And so we have the breezy, heathery heights of Thurstaston Common and Caldy Hill across which we are free to roam, and lots of other, smaller patches of 'wild-ish' Wirral. But the old local authorities did their bit too by creating many parks (both urban and semi-urban), which today are essential and much-loved bits of greenery, often in or near places which need them most.

*Hill Bark set amidst the rugged open spaces of Royden Park.*

*A beech avenue, Arrowe Park.*

Birkenhead boasts one of the oldest public parks in the country. Designed by Sir Joseph Paxton, the celebrated landscape gardener, it was opened in 1847 'amidst scenes of great rejoicing and celebration' with its 225 acres of 'extensive drives, beautiful walks and elegant gardens, adorned with groves, fountains, ornamental waters and numerous sources of pleasure'. The Park has recently undergone a much-needed and richly deserved multi-million-pound facelift.

Arrowe Country Park embraces the former Arrowe Park. Although sadly built upon for the hospital on its eastern side, the Park is still a lovely oasis amidst the bricks and mortar of this part of Wirral. The Arrowe estate was laid out around the Hall in the 1830s by John Ralph Shaw, a wealthy Liverpool warehouse owner and a keen huntsman. He it was who planted the fine woodlands we enjoy today, and dammed up the Arrowe Brook to form the lovely lake and waterfall at the western edge of the Park.

The Park knew international fame for two glorious, muddy weeks in July 1929 when it hosted the Scouts' World Jamboree. Over 50,000 scouts converged on Arrowe from all over the world during one of the wettest summer spells of the century. The Jamboree became the Mudboree, with special raised walkways being erected over the worst-affected areas. However, spirits remained high, and it was stated that much of the Jamboree's success was because of the spirit of comradeship generated by the awful conditions!

These are the big parks, the big open spaces. But explore other, perhaps lesser-known places: Burton Woods, Dibbinsdale, Brotherton Park, Rivacre Valley, Stanney Woods, and many others. They are all little oases of wildness surviving in an increasingly urban peninsula.

*The Boathouse, Birkenhead Park.*

*Barn owl.*

The wealth and variety of different habitats ensures that the Wirral Peninsula is rich in wildlife. It has woodlands, small streams and miles of hedgerows; an impressive coastline with crumbly cliffs, sandy beaches and grassy dunes; two estuaries of international importance for bird life, with mud-flats and salt-marsh; an offshore island with its associated cliffs, rocky bays and inter-tidal shores; and, of course, windswept heaths, pools, ponds and pits, and a few grassy meadows.

Highlights for me are the springtime carpets of bluebells in our ancient woods; the majesty of the gorse on the heathlands of Caldy and Thurstaston hills; the coastal flowers of high summer on the sand-dunes of Red Rocks and Moreton; the late-summer show of heathers on the high commons; and the autumn tints of October on the old trees in our parks and woods.

Birds abound here, for the long coastline with its cliffs, beaches, marshes and mudflats offers an ornithological delight. Especially appealing are the spring and autumnal flocks of migrant birds flying in their thousands over the wide, wet expanses of the estuaries and sand-banks.

The sea also provides a safe haven for the colony of grey seals, hauled out on the sandbanks beyond Hilbre Island.

'The Dee is an estuary of many moods. The tranquillity of a June day when the summer tide creeps over the sun-baked sands with scarcely a ripple and the Welsh mountains lie hidden beneath the soft veil of a heat haze – can this be the same sea that, in autumn, floods the estuary with a carpet of angry grey water, whipped to foam by a west wind, breaking in showers of spray over my bird island?'
**Guy Farrar, 1938**

*Tide-washed Hilbre Island in the Dee Estuary.*

*Wader flocks at Hoylake.*

*Raby Mere, a long-time favourite beauty spot in the middle of Wirral.*

*Sunset over Hilbre Island.*